Patterns

by Craig Hammersmith

Content and Reading Adviser: Mary Beth Fletcher, Ed.D.
Educational Consultant/Reading Specialist
The Carroll School, Lincoln, Massachusetts

COMPASS POINT BOOKS

Minneapolis, Minnesota

Compass Point Books
3109 West 50th Street, #115
Minneapolis, MN 55410

Visit Compass Point Books on the Internet at *www.compasspointbooks.com*
or e-mail your request to *custserv@compasspointbooks.com*

Photographs ©: Laura Doss/Corbis, cover; Kent & Donna Dannen, 4; Unicorn Stock Photos/Richard Gilbert, 5; Cheryl A. Ertelt, 6, 7 (bottom); PhotoDisc, 7 (top), 15, 20; Scott Berner/Visuals Unlimited, 8; Unicorn Stock Photos/Frank Pennington, 9 (top); Unicorn Stock Photos/ChromoSohm/Sohm, 9 (bottom); Ariel Skelley/Corbis, 10; Richard Hutchings/Corbis, 11; Norvia Behling, 12; Jose Luis Pelaez, Inc./Corbis, 13; Eric R. Berndt/The Image Finders, 14; John Gerlach/Visuals Unlimited, 16; Francesc Muntada/Corbis, 17; John D. Cunningham/Visuals Unlimited, 18; Photo Network/Patti McConville, 19; RubberBall Productions, 21 (top left); Comstock, 21 (top right); U.S. Department of Agriculture, 21 (bottom).

Project Manager: Rebecca Weber McEwen
Editors: Heidi Schoof and Patricia Stockland
Photo Researcher: Svetlana Zhurkina
Designer: Jaime Martens

Library of Congress Cataloging-in-Publication Data
Hammersmith, Craig.
  Patterns / by Craig Hammersmith.
    p. cm. — (Spyglass books)
Summary: Shows how to make patterns, how to find patterns
such as checkerboards and polka-dots, and how common
patterns are in nature.
Includes bibliographical references and index.
  ISBN 0-7565-0452-X (hardcover)
  1. Pattern perception—Juvenile literature.   [1. Pattern
perception.]   I. Title. II. Series.
  BF294.H36 2003
  152.14'23—dc21   2002012627

Contents

NOTE: Glossary words are in **bold** the first time they appear.

What Is a Pattern?

A pattern is a bunch of colors or shapes that *repeat* over and over again.

Did You Know?
Footprints can make a pattern.

Lots of Stripes

Zebras have a pattern.
Can you see the pattern
in these zebras?

Did You Know?

The black and white pattern of stripes may help zebras hide from *predators.*

Crazy Quilts

Quilts have patterns.
Can you see the pattern
in this quilt?

People *sew* together different pieces of *fabric* to make special quilt patterns.

Fancy Pants

Some clothes have patterns. Can you see the pattern in this dress?

Staying Safe

Bright colors are easy to find if someone gets lost. They can be seen by people in cars, which helps a person stay safe along a road.

Let's Play

Checkerboards have a pattern. Can you see the pattern in this checkerboard?

Checkerboards have a pattern of squares to show players where to put their checkers.

How Corny!

Cornfields have a pattern. Can you see the pattern in this cornfield?

Sometimes, farmers make a *maze* in their cornfields where people can play and hide.

Spiderwebs

Some spiderwebs have patterns. Can you see the pattern in this spiderweb?

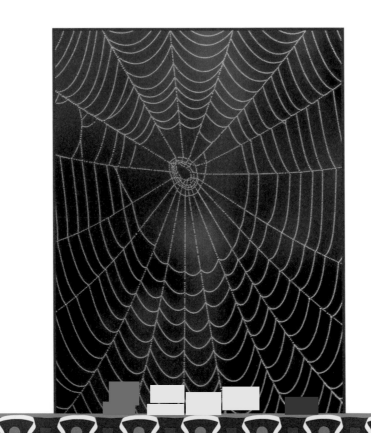

Did You Know?

Spiders make webs with patterns to help make the webs strong.

Building Blocks

Some houses have patterns. Can you see the pattern in these bricks?

Builders *stack* bricks in patterns to make houses as strong as possible.

Patterns All Around

Some things have patterns to make them stronger or better. Some things have patterns just to look good.

There are patterns all around us.

Glossary

fabric–cloth or material

maze–a complicated pattern of paths or lines, made as a puzzle to find your way through

predators–animals that hunt other animals for food

repeat–to say or do something again

sew–to make or attach something using stitches from a needle and thread

stack–to pile things up, one on top of another

Learn More

Books

Harris, Trudy. *Pattern Fish.* Brookfield, Conn.: Millbrook Press, 2000.

Koomen, Michele. *Patterns: What Comes Next?* Mankato, Minn.: Bridgestone Books, 2001.

Swinburne, Stephen R. *Lots and Lots of Zebra Stripes: Patterns in Nature.* Honesdale, Pa.: Boyds Mills Press, 1998.

Web Sites

Pattern Blocks
http://ejad.best.vwh.net/java/patterns/
Pattern Mania
www.primarygames.com/patterns/start.htm

Index

GR: G
Word Count: 122

From Craig Hammersmith

I like to camp in the mountains near my Colorado home. I always bring a good book and a flashlight so I can read in the tent!

6/6/04